CONDUCTING A NEEDS ANALYSIS

Geri McArdle, Ph.D.

A FIFTY-MINUTE™ SERIES BOOK

This Fifty-Minute™ book is designed to be "read with a pencil." It is an excellent workbook for self-study as well as classroom learning. All material is copyright-protected and cannot be duplicated without permission from the publisher. *Therefore, be sure to order a copy for every training participant by contacting:*

CRISP. Learning
Menlo Park, California

1-800-442-7477

CrispLearning.com

CONDUCTING A NEEDS ANALYSIS

Geri McArdle, Ph.D.

CREDITS
Managing Editor: **Kathleen Barcos**
Editor: **Regina Preciado**
Production: **Barbara Atmore**
Typesetting: **ExecuStaff**
Cover Design: **Carol Harris**
Artwork: **Ralph Mapson**

© 1998 by Crisp Publications, Inc.
Printed in the United States of America by Von Hoffmann Graphics, Inc.

CrispLearning.com

00 01 02 03   10 9 8 7 6 5 4 3 2

Library of Congress Catalog Card Number 97-77977
McArdle, Geri
Conducting a Needs Analysis
ISBN 1-56052-423-5

This book is printed on recyclable paper with soy ink.

LEARNING OBJECTIVES FOR:

CONDUCTING A NEEDS ANALYSIS

The objectives for *Conducting a Needs Analysis* are listed below. They have been developed to guide you, the reader, to the core issues covered in this book.

Objectives

❑ 1) **To discuss reasons for a needs analysis and pre-planning**

❑ 2) **To explain investigation and data development**

❑ 3) **To show how to analyze data and evaluate training possibilities**

❑ 4) **To discuss the needs analysis report**

Assessing Your Progress

In addition to the learning objectives, Crisp Learning has developed an **assessment** that covers the fundamental information presented in this book. A twenty-five item, multiple choice/true-false question-naire allows the reader to evaluate his or her comprehension of the subject matter. An answer sheet with a chart matching the questions to the listed objectives is also available. To learn how to obtain a copy of this assessment, please call **1-800-442-7477** and ask to speak with a Customer Service Representative.

Assessments should not be used in any selection process.

ABOUT THE AUTHOR

Geri McArdle, Ph.D., is managing director of Training Systems Institute, a training consulting group. She is an international award-winning author and Outstanding Faculty Member (1989) at The Johns Hopkins University and a postdoctoral fellow at Harvard University.

Dr. McArdle has also produced public service television programs, and she is a frequent international lecturer and guest faculty member teaching faculty and physicians. The other books she has written for Crisp Publications include *Delivering Effective Training Sessions* and *Developing Instructional Designs.*

ABOUT THE SERIES

With over 200 titles in print, the acclaimed Crisp 50-Minute™ series presents self-paced learning at its easiest and best. These comprehensive self-study books for business or personal use are filled with exercises, activities, assessments, and case studies that capture your interest and increase your understanding.

Other Crisp products, based on the 50-Minute books, are available in a variety of learning style formats for both individual and group study, including audio, video, CD-ROM, and computer-based training.

CONTENTS

CONTENTS (continued)

Introduction

WHAT IS A NEEDS ANALYSIS?

The **needs analysis process** is a series of activities conducted to identify problems or other issues in the workplace and to determine whether training is an appropriate response. A needs analysis is usually the first in a series of steps implemented to encourage effective change. This is mainly because a needs analysis specifically defines the gaps between current and desired organizational and individual performances.

WHO CONDUCTS A NEEDS ANALYSIS AND WHY?

An in-house trainer or a consultant performs a needs analysis to collect and document information concerning any of the following three issues:

- Performance problems
- The anticipated introduction of a new system, task or technology
- A desire by the organization to benefit from a perceived opportunity

In all three situations, the starting point is a desire to effect change. Given this, you must know how the people who will experience change perceive it. In the absence of a needs analysis, you may find employees resistant to change and training. They may be unable to transfer their newly acquired skills to their jobs because of organizational constraints.

A needs analysis often reveals the need for well-targeted training, and that is the focus of this book. However, keep in mind that training is not always the best way to try to close a particular gap between a company's goals and its actual performance. Those conducting the analysis must get a clear idea of the problem, look at possible remedies and report on their findings to management before deciding on the best solution.

When properly done, a needs analysis is a wise investment for the organization. It saves time, money and effort by working on the right problems. Organizations that fail to support needs analyses make costly mistakes: they use training when another method would have been more effective; they use too much or too little training; or they use training, but fail to follow up on it. A well-performed analysis provides the information that can lead to solutions that focus on the areas of greatest need.

The process of conducting a needs analysis is a systematic one based on specific information-gathering techniques. A needs analysis proceeds in stages, with the findings of one stage affecting and helping to shape the next. There is no easy formula for carrying out this process. Each particular situation requires its own mix of observing, probing, analyzing and deducing. In many ways, the needs analysis is like detective work: you follow up on every lead, check every piece of information and examine every alternative before drawing any conclusions. Only then can you be sure you have the evidence on which to base a sound strategy for problem solving.

A needs analysis is not a one-time event. Many companies administer needs analyses at regular intervals, usually every year or two.

WHAT IS A LEARNING ORGANIZATION?

The objective of the needs analysis is to get people to work at optimal levels. Many managers assume that an average performer's work is the standard and that a high performer's work is exceptional. In many workplaces, managers typically believe that the high achiever is a workaholic, is lucky, or possesses a unique talent. However, if an organization establishes an ideal that involves an exceptional—but achievable—level of performance and then asks, "What if everyone could perform at this level?" the exceptional can become the standard. An organization that sets a vision and establishes objectives to become a "learning organization" is one that asks this question.

A learning organization uses its resources most effectively. When an organization adopts this philosophy, all performance is targeted around the organization's core goals, all employees assume individual responsibility for their work objectives and everyone respects individual values. This type of organization has plenty of scope for trainers, who have opportunities to assess employees' skills and to provide management with guidance to keep the organization abreast of the rapid changes occurring in business and technology, while at the same time establishing a baseline for continuous performance improvement.

SIX POINTS TO REMEMBER

Here are the six points to bear in mind to reach a successful conclusion when conducting your needs analysis.

① Involve Management Early

Often management is the driving force behind a needs analysis. If you do not already have management's support, get it. Conducting a needs analysis in an environment that fosters mutual respect and honesty will allow you to better reach an agreement about the outcome.

② Training May Not Be the Answer

Providing training simply because management requires it does not guarantee success. You must decide if the issue is a training one. You must also establish how the proposed training affects the proposed audience; the likely audience's, supervisors', and management's acceptance; and the training's effect on the entire organization.

③ The Big Picture

Keep in mind:

1. Why do people perform or not perform well?

2. What performance is desired?

④ Look At All Influential Factors

The work environment is an important factor in the needs analysis process. So, too, is examining in detail individuals' skills, knowledge and attitudes about their tasks, jobs, bosses and the organization. Together, these factors influence your decision about whether to provide a training program.

⑤ Training ⊉ Education

Education programs, like a company's orientation session, provide general knowledge. Everyone receives the same information regardless of whether it applies to each individual's situation.

Training, on the other hand, focuses on job-specific skills. The trainer teaches only those employees who need to learn new information and shows them how to apply what they learn. The employees can implement their new knowledge immediately.

⑥ Performance Standards and Criteria

Establishing standards of excellence and using them as performance criteria is basic to an organization. Use the following three indicators to measure individual and organizational performance:

- What does the organization consider baseline skills?

- What level of performance is expected of the individuals, groups, departments and organization?

- What behaviors and attitudes exist among employees and management?

STEPS TO A NEEDS ANALYSIS

This book will help guide you through the needs analysis process. Following these steps will help you see where problems exist, determine whether training would be appropriate to fix the problems and outline a training course.

The steps in this process are:

> **STEP** ① **Surveillance**
>
> **STEP** ② **Investigation**
>
> **STEP** ③ **Analysis**
>
> **STEP** ④ **Report**

While this is a step-by-step approach, every organization's situation is different. You will need to be flexible and willing to adjust your methods if needed. Good luck!

S T E P

I

Surveillance

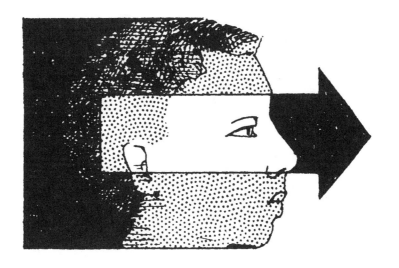

☑ WHAT IS THE CURRENT SITUATION?

A needs analysis begins with a snapshot of the current circumstances. You probably won't need a telephoto lens for this part of the process, but you do need to look closely and objectively at both the operations and the people that the coming changes will affect. Once you have a clear picture of what needs to change in order to improve, you can assemble your helpers and continue with the needs analysis.

☑ DEFINE THE NEEDS AND IDENTIFY PERFORMANCE GAPS

Before embarking on a needs analysis, you need an accurate idea of the problems involved. What results does the organization currently achieve and how do they compare with the expected organizational results? If a performance problem is involved, how has performance changed from the past? What is the desired performance?

Use the worksheet on page 13 to make an initial assessment of current and desired results. You will gather more detailed data later on, in Step 2: Investigation. For now, concentrate on identifying needs, not developing solutions.

Of course, you can't see all of the needs by yourself. You will need to observe the day-to-day operations of the organization and interact with people at all levels, from production line to management. Find out how they feel and what they know about the organization, their work and their environment. Let them voice their concerns. What do they perceive as strengths? What barriers prevent them from reaching their potential?

Look for trends. When you compare the organization's needs with the employees' perceptions, the issues will emerge. The Interview Guide on page 14 will help you track each employee's response.

During surveillance you should regularly review the situation in your organization. Automatically circulated documents that provide state-of-the-organization themes or issues will give you an up-to-date and broad picture of what is happening, and you can begin scanning for performance problems and training opportunities.

In addition, make an effort to maintain informal contacts with individuals throughout the organization. Regularly assess the attitudes and feelings of the organization's staff, even if your assessment is subjective. Stay abreast of all policies, procedures and standards relating to work performance.

Without the overall picture, you could overemphasize one need at the expense of others, resulting in a less than optimal use of resources and a loss of credibility.

Identifying Needs and Performance Gaps

Area	What is happening?	What should be happening?
Organization's mission, objectives		
Performance standards		
Budget targets		
Job descriptions		
Production		
Performance appraisals		
Labor turnover		
Absenteeism		
Accidents		
Disciplinary actions		
Labor costs		
Cost of materials		
Overtime		
Economic predictions		
Technical development		
Legal issues		
Other		

14

INTERVIEW GUIDE: Step ① : Surveillance

1. What problem/s do you see within the organization?

_____

_____

2. How many times have you observed this situation?

❑   ❑   ❑   ❑

_1–3_   _4–6_   _7–10_   _More than 10_

3. What type of problem is it?

❑   ❑   ❑   ❑

Performance   _Knowledge_   _Skill_   _Behavior_

4. What is the extent of the problem?

❑   ❑   ❑   ❑

Macro   _Micro (1)_   _Micro (2)_   _Micro (3)_
(Entire   _(More than one_   _(Single_   _(Individual)_
organization)   _department)_   _department)_

5. Who are the stakeholders?

_____   _____

_____   _____

6. Area and times of observation

Area	_Date_	_Time_
_____	_____	_____
_____	_____	_____

In collaboration with Vicki Gridley, Brisbane, Queensland, Australia.

☑ ORGANIZE A TASK FORCE

Formally and informally gathering input from various constituencies is critical to your needs analysis. You might want to create a permanent task force that includes representatives from each department you call upon to guide, verify and support your actions on an ongoing basis. When you select your team, choose those who know and care about the situation and those who do not care but should. Also, try to identify a contact person or "champion" who is committed to training and whom you can call upon for support and resources. You will need this support later to get through critical points in the needs analysis process.

☑ ORGANIZE THE DATA

The next step is to organize the information you have gathered so far.

- Sort the information into categories.

- Separate training issues from nontraining issues. For example, some problems might be related to a policy issue such as the firm's compensation procedures.

- Identify content or training topic issues.

- Determine whether an issue is a hands-on skill issue.

For the most part, training needs are performance-related, such as helping employees do their present jobs better, orienting new employees or keeping employees informed of technical and procedural changes. Some training activities also provide employees with an opportunity to develop their skills and knowledge, usually in connection with performance-related needs.

Needs can be divided into two classes: micro and macro. A **micro** need is one that exists for just one person or for a very small population. A **macro** need is one that exists for a large group of employees, frequently for the entire population with the same job classifications.

Examples of Micro and Macro Needs	
Micro Needs	**Macro Needs**
A new employee needs to understand what is expected of him or her on the job.	All employees need orientation when the company opens a new building.
A three-person unit has micro-computers installed and all three are expected to know how to operate them.	All employees are expected to be able to use a newly installed, company-wide computer system.
A supervisor is having problems managing his or her time.	All first-line supervisors have been asked to initiate performance appraisal discussions in their units.

Dugan Laird, *Approaches to Training and Development*, Reading, MA: Addison-Wesley, 1985.

☑ DEVELOP PRIORITIES

It is time to set priorities for the various needs you have identified. You can do this by ranking needs based on the cost of meeting the need versus the cost of ignoring it. Alternatively, you can carry out a cost-benefit analysis for each need or cluster of needs you have discovered. Use these questions to help sort the data you gathered during the preliminary investigation:

What will a solution cost?
How much time will the solution take?
What is the cost of ignoring the problem?

This information is essential to winning support for any solution. Senior management will be interested in the effect on the bottom line and the overall contribution to the organization. Line managers will be interested in evaluating solutions based on their costs in terms of lost or delayed production, employees' time and possible overtime. Remember, little will be accomplished without management support.

Once you have identified and developed a priority list of the needs and possible solutions, you must then conduct a "sanity check" to make sure your assumptions are on target. Call on your task force or team up with members of the organization to make sure you have accurately assessed the situation.

☑ MEET WITH MANAGEMENT

By now you have a good idea of where performance gaps are occurring. But before you begin investigating them further, you must present your initial findings to management. Management should review the priorities list and make the necessary changes, and you should work together to plan the next stages of the needs analysis.

This meeting is of the utmost importance. Without management's commitment to the project, your needs analysis will waste both time and money.

Your primary goal before the meeting is to develop a well-defined problem statement. The Sample Premeeting Guide on page 19 will help you organize your presentation. As you prepare, consider the following four factors:

1. TIME

The analysis is a planned process that takes time to design, develop and conduct depending on the complexity of the situation.

2. NEED

Because the assessment process does take time and resources, you must convince management that this process is necessary and is an investment (the biggest required agreement here is cooperation).

3. TIMELINESS

Often the assessment process takes place over unreasonable time lines. Make sure that you develop an appropriate plan for conducting and reporting. Don't promise anything you can't develop because of time constraints.

4. CAUSE AND EFFECT

Look for situations in which one situation affects another and for root causes. Separate problems from symptoms.

When you have your material ready, schedule the meeting. Don't forget to invite other staff if appropriate.

PREMEETING GUIDE
Needs Assessment Client Meeting #1:
Premeeting Information

Date/Time: _____

Place: _____

Contact/Position: _____

Issue(s):

Guiding Questions or Topics:

Suggested Next Steps:

MEET WITH MANAGEMENT (continued)

The Meeting Guide on page 21 will help you record the decisions you and management reach. During this meeting, you must:

- Define the task.

- Agree on the need(s).

- State the desired outcome.

- Establish shared responsibility.

- Identify a contact person for the report.

- Record management's commitment to proceed.

MEETING GUIDE	
Needs Assessment Meeting #1: Meeting Guidelines	

Date/Time: _____

Place: _____

Contact/Position: _____

About the Target Task	**Responses**
• Organization's performance standards	
• Work conditions	
• Supervisor's performance expectations	
About the Participants	**Responses**
• Stated training need(s)	
• Current performance level(s)	
• Current level(s) of knowledge	
• Attitudes toward task	
• Attitudes toward training	
About the Training Session	**Responses**
• Time frame for planning	
• Stakeholders	
• Conditions under which training will be conducted	
• Available resources (e.g., materials, tools)	
• Instructor's skills	

☑ WRITE SUMMARY MEMO

As soon as possible after the initial meeting, complete the postmeeting summary memo. The memo should request written commitment to continue the needs assessment, state agreed-upon allocation of resources and training outcomes and establish a project time line that outlines all the steps in the needs process. Use the analysis Client Summary Memorandum below as a template.

Client Summary Memorandum

MEMORANDUM

To: Client

From: Trainer/Facilitator

Date: June 24, 1998

Analysis Subject: Needs Analysis Meeting

1. Statement of the Problem

Write a clear statement describing the assessment and training outcomes mutually agreed upon during the meeting.

2. Description of Tasks

Define the task you perceived to be involved in the needs analysis process.

3. Summary of Analyses

Summarize the information about the target tasks, the participants and the training situation. This will help management make a commitment to the process and the proposed training outcome.

4. Proposed Plan

Present your plan for conducting the analysis, including tasks, time line and a project budget.

5. Request for Management's Commitment

Request written commitment to the project.

Exercise

Check true or false or fill in the blank.

1. One of the advantages of a needs analysis is that you can compare where you are with where you want to go.

    ❏ True   ❏ False

2. The needs analysis process looks at how a task is currently performed and considers how it should be performed.

    ❏ True   ❏ False

3. The first stage of the process is similar to _____ work.

4. Informal contacts or networks are of no value during the course of collecting data for your assessment.

    ❏ True   ❏ False

5. The needs assessment process is always lengthy, expensive and requires rigid adherence to formal procedural guidelines.

    ❏ True   ❏ False

6. What is your definition of needs analysis?

7. Once a problem is identified, you must decide whether it is a macro or micro issue. What's the difference between the two categories?

CASE STUDY: Step ① *Surveillance*

Club Hoopla is a resort company. Established in 1992 by a group of U.S. investors, it currently owns six resorts (two in the Caribbean, one in Florida, and three in Mexico) and is headquartered in Miami. Originally, the club catered only to adults. However, in 1996, two of the resorts started accepting children as young as three months in an effort to keep up with the growing demand for upscale family vacations.

Lorraine Tersolt oversees staff training for all the clubs. Recently, the following problems have come to her attention.

- *Lack of language capabilities among resort staff.* The Florida club attracts a great many Europeans because of its location close to Orlando and the trips it organizes to the area's attractions. Many Europeans also visit the Caribbean clubs. In addition, the Mexican clubs have become popular among visitors from other Latin American countries.

- *Complaints by some guests that the clubs that cater to children are no longer appropriate for adults* vacationing without children.

- One of the clubs' attractions is that visitors can participate in a number of sports. The club provides all equipment and instruction. However, *some of the instructors are not sufficiently well versed in their sports and their equipment is shoddy,* especially in those clubs that specialize in scuba diving, where safety is of particular importance.

- Another specialty of the clubs is a nightly show put on by the staff. *The staff complain that they are too tired to perform properly* and that rehearsals are held after the nightly shows, sometimes lasting until two o'clock in the morning.

Lorraine must separate the training and nontraining issues. Before meeting with the Training Committee—management and staff members she appointed to help design, develop and deliver training at Club Hoopla—she develops an action plan to guide the process.

Phase 1 of her action plan is to prepare a well-defined problem statement for the Training Committee's review. Using the Training Needs Worksheet to help organize her findings, she gathers the data from newsletters, guest activity reports, summaries of adult and children's programs and other written material. She also identifies key individuals at each site whom she will interview to get their perspectives of the problems. She makes sure to include a variety of people, from management to staff to guests.

After completing this preliminary research and reviewing the files she has kept throughout the surveillance stage, Lorraine will have an accurate idea of the areas where training is appropriate. She can then move on to the next step of the needs analysis process: Investigation.

BOX 3.1 Training Needs Worksheet

1. Outline on the following table your sources of training needs and ideas. Be as specific as possible in identifying these sources, including such items as names of individuals and particular groups and titles of reports and documents, and note the location of the sources.

Source	Internal to organization	External to organization
People Job Organization		

2. Based on the material you outlined in the table, make a list of those sources you would use first, second and third. Are there any you would choose not to use at this time?

Sources you would use first:

Sources you would use second:

Sources you would use third:

Sources you would choose not to use at this time:

S T E P

II

Investigation

INITIATING THE INVESTIGATION

In Step 1: Surveillance, you observed the situation closely enough to determine whether a performance-related problem exists. Now you will gather further data to establish whether training is an appropriate response. This data will also provide the foundation upon which you will build an effective training program.

Use the following questions to help establish some investigative parameters:

1. What results does the organization seek?

2. How do these results compare with the organization's key objectives?

3. What contribution does the training department need to make to meet the organization's key objectives?

4. What method(s) are currently in use to set priorities and justify training targets?

5. How are training results measured?

☑ IDENTIFY THE DATA YOU NEED

The outcome of a needs analysis will only be as good as the data you collect. Furthermore, you can use the data for other purposes long after you have used it to determine training needs; it may help you avoid reinventing the wheel in future endeavors.

First, establish your goals. What do you expect your needs analysis to find based on your preliminary research and findings during Surveillance? List your expectations and note the conditions prior to assessment.

Second, understand your reporting needs. At what levels should you gather data? Data collected for a needs analysis should be pertinent to the organizational levels the issue affects: the entire organization, sub-units and individuals. Specifying the reporting levels early on enables you to collect information at a sufficient level of detail.

Third, identify "content" areas of needs analysis: the **organization, task or job, and people** components. Most applications of needs analysis emphasize the person component, ignoring the critical roles of the organization and job components. However, training needs are generated from all three sources.

In the content-level matrix, the intersection of each content factor with each organizational level suggests questions or issues that a comprehensive approach to needs analysis should address. The framework is useful for identifying factors that can influence performance and provides a guide to what kinds of data you will be considering.

Content-Level Matrix		
CONTENT (FACTORS TO CONSIDER)		
Person	**Task/Job**	**Organization**
Individual • Knowledge • Skills • Abilities • Motivations • Attitudes	• Task requirements • Technology used to perform task • Tools/equipment • Financial/ budgetary support • Services and help from others • Personal preparation needed (education, training, experience) • Physical comfort	• Goals, objectives and values • Concept of how work should be scheduled or coordinated • Individual's understanding of role vs. organization's expectations
Sub-unit • Quality of interpersonal relations • Collective/team skills • Climate	• Tasks performed by unit • Technology used by unit • Do workgroup norms constrain or promote each individual's performance?	• Goals, objectives and values of unit as a whole • Short-term vs. long-term outlook
Organization • Skills • Climate • Degree of participation in decision making	• Tasks performed by everyone in the company • Technology used by everyone in the company • Availability of resources such as materials, supplies and information	• Goals, objectives and values from the top • Approaches to scheduling, coordination and time allocation • Effectiveness of reaching goals

☑ EVALUATE KEY DATA SOURCES

When conducting your investigation, you will collect information from several sources. You will encounter two types of data: hard and soft. Hard data is factual and objective, found in reports, accounting records and other official documentation. Soft data is subjective and comes from group discussions, individual interviews and opinion questionnaires.

The chart below highlights the pros and cons of the most common sources of data.

Comparison of Key Data Sources			
Source	Description	Advantage	Disadvantage
Human Resource records	Contemporary, ongoing documentation of the causes of performance problems and training issues	Objective	Time consuming
Accident and safety reports	Reveal clusters of issue types by department and position	Quantitative	Doesn't necessarily identify causes
Grievance filings and turnover rates	Shows problems with employees or immediate supervisors	Documentation	Issues may be related to policy rather than to training
Performance evaluation and merit ratings	Measured analysis of employees on absolute and relative bases	Documents skills and employee progress	Subjective, based on supervisors opinions as well as observations
Production statistics	Numerical results of output and itemized costs of doing business	Quantitative	Doesn't always provide a complete picture

☑ SELECT DATA COLLECTION METHODS

In conducting your needs analysis, you can collect data from sources such as questionnaires, interviews, observations, focus groups, documentation, job descriptions, and policies and procedures. As you proceed, remember that you must clearly define a problem before you can solve it. Some tips for doing so:

> ✓ Ask *who*, *what*, *why*, *when* and *how* questions.
>
> ✓ Develop a clear and concise problem statement.
>
> ✓ Document causes of the problem.
>
> ✓ Identify feelings about the problem.
>
> ✓ Determine who is involved and why.
>
> ✓ Separate facts from opinions.

CONDUCTING EFFECTIVE INTERVIEWS

You can talk to individuals in person or by telephone. The advantages of interviews are that in addition to providing information, they can reveal feelings, opinions and unexpected insights or suggestions, including potential solutions to problems. Disadvantages of using this technique include time and labor. In addition, good results depend on an unbiased interviewer who listens well and who does not judge, interrupt or distort responses.

The five main types of interviews are:

1. *Unstructured*

Exploratory, only the area of interest is chosen for discussion, interviewers "follow their instincts" in formulating and ordering questions.

2. *Partially structured*

Interviewers choose an area for discussion and formulate questions, but the order is up to the interviewer. Interviewers may add questions or modify them as they deem appropriate. Questions are open-ended, and responses are recorded almost verbatim, possibly taped.

3. *Semistructured*

The questions and their order of presentation are predetermined and open-ended. Interviewers record the essence of each response.

4. *Structured*

Questions are predetermined and interviewers code responses as they are given.

5. *Totally structured*

Questions, order and coding are predetermined. Respondents are presented with alternatives for each answer so that the phrasing of responses is structured.

Computer-assisted telephone interviews use a computer to guide the respondent through the questions. The interview begins with a series of questions that determines whether the person who answered the phone is part of the targeted sample. The computer is programmed to terminate the call if the person is not from the target group.

Telephone interviews tend to elicit shorter responses than face-to-face encounters. Computer-assisted telephone interviews have some of the same advantages of face-to-face interviews and should be the method of choice when results must be obtained in a short period of time.

However, many people are put off by electronic interviewers, so be sure to evaluate the attitudes of your potential interviewees before committing yourself. You may decide to spend the money and time on person-to-person phone interviews, especially if your target sample is small. Either way, the worksheet on page 36 will help to organize the process.

CONDUCTING EFFECTIVE INTERVIEWS
(continued)

Model Telephone Interview Guide

Project: _____

Respondent's Name: _____

Position: _____

Location: _____ Telephone Number: _____

Date Interview Conducted: _____ Interviewer: _____

Opening Statement: Hello, my name is _____ and I will be conducting the training session on Monday. I would like to talk with you for a few minutes about your expectations for the seminar. Is this a convenient time? (This is also the point when you describe how the information will be used, if the respondent will be anonymous in the report, who will see the data, etc.)

Demographic Information: Before we start, I'd like to get a bit of information from you for our statistical analysis (demographic variables printed here).

Interview Questions: In general, what would you say is important for the group to cover during the session?

Closing Statement: Thank you again for your time. Are there any final comments you would like to add?

WORKING WITH FOCUS GROUPS

Focus groups consist of multiple interviews with different small groups. Focus groups can help determine the significance of a particular situation to various individuals, find the needed range of alternatives for closed-end questions, or determine how people feel about an issue or product.

Focus groups are most successful with a relatively small, homogeneous group. One of the disadvantages of this method is that it is difficult to assemble the right mix of people; if your group is widely diverse, some members may withdraw. Another hurdle is finding a time that fits every-one's schedule. Once you do get everyone together, using a circular seating arrangement facilitates spontaneous responses and interchange.

To make the most of your focus group:

- Limit the group to 12 people.

- Use a structured guide for the discussion.

- Have one facilitator responsible for taking notes or recording responses on a flip chart.

- Tape responses if you can do so unobtrusively.

- Arrange a group where participants do not report to one another (no supervisors present).

- Use a variety of group facilitation tools (e.g., brainstorming, listing by priority) to stimulate responses.

OBSERVING THE WORKFLOW

You can use observations to find out what happens while employees are working. This method helps to obtain information on optimal and actual performance and to infer the cause(s) of performance problems. The advantage is that, like interviews, observations are flexible. Observations can also enlighten you about the context in which performance takes place and provide valuable nonverbal information about what goes on at work that may not coincide with people's verbal opinions.

Some disadvantages of observations are that you can affect the setting and the way people do their jobs. Naturally, you will also bring biases to the situation, thus gathering information subjectively rather than objectively.

In addition, the use of a guide is essential. The guide should be easy to understand and use. As you prepare it, keep in mind the purposes of the observation. Limit its scope to the specific aspect of work on which you are concentrating, and allow room for both qualitative and quantitative information. Your guide must also serve as a blueprint for followup.

Because you must prepare your guide ahead of time, you might overlook useful information, so be sure to leave plenty of space for additional comments. Do not dwell on impressions. *Go for facts.*

You can take either management's suggestion about whom to observe or you can use a random sample. Your observations can be covert or overt. If you choose to do a covert observation, which is the most common, you should introduce yourself and then fade into the background.

To conduct successful observations:

- Identify ahead of time what performance aspect you plan to observe.

- Familiarize yourself with the job or system you will observe.

- Design and use an effective observation guide.

- Choose an observation method that will provide valid results.

- Blend into the environment. Observation should be an unobtrusive activity.

- Be patient. Sometimes observation work can be tedious.

- Consider both the big picture and the details.

- Follow up. Immediately after an observation, review your guide and notes.

Advantages and Disadvantages of Observation		
Observation	Advantages	Disadvantages
• May be as technical as time-motion studies or as functionally or behaviorally specific as observing new board or staff members interact during a meeting. • May be as unstructured as walking through an agency's offices on the lookout for evidence of communication barriers. • May be used normatively to distinguish between effective and ineffective behaviors, organizational structures and/or process.	• Minimizes interruption of routine work flow or group activity. • Generates *in situ* data, highly relevant to the situation where response to identified training needs/ interests will impact. • Provides important comparison checks between the observer's and the respondent's inferences (when combined with a feedback step).	• Requires a highly skilled observer with both process and content knowledge (unlike an interviewer, who needs, for the most part, only process skills). • Carries limitations because able to collect data only within the work setting (flip side of the first advantage).

STUDY OFFICIAL DOCUMENTS

Several types of organizational documents can provide information about employees. For example, personnel files, accident reports and reports of customer complaints can help you establish the level of employees' skills and knowledge.

Using documents has several advantages. Mainly, they are an inexpensive needs analysis tool because the company has already collected the information.

The disadvantages of using documents are (1) they are not necessarily complete because you are dealing with the viewpoints of the people who prepared the documentation, so you must be careful not to generalize from the information you gather, and (2) they may be difficult to obtain.

You should be working closely with the HR manager throughout this process. It is up to him or her to establish whether it is appropriate for you to see certain records. For example, reviewing performance appraisals may help you identify performance gaps, but those records are confidential and HR may decide not to release them.

For effective use of documents:

- Explain clearly why you need each document.

- Prepare to make a case for the need to review documents.

- Describe how you will ensure that confidentiality is preserved.

- Review all relevant documents from a random sample.

- Examine documents twice, first to gain a broad perspective, and second to identify all relevant aspects of performance.

- Decide whether it would be useful to share general impressions with the manager who provided access to the documents.

☑ OBTAIN MANAGEMENT'S APPROVAL TO PROCEED

Make sure you have received a written response to paragraph five of the Client Summary Memorandum that requests management's commitment to the project. Request that your contact give further evidence of this commitment in a brief letter.

You may offer the Sample Client Commitment Letter as an example, if needed.

Sample Client Commitment Letter

XYZ Company • 1000 10th Street
City, State, Zip Code • Area Code Phone Number

June 30, 1998
Ms. Dew Wright
Human Resources Director
XYX Company
1000 10th Street
City, State, Zip Code

Dear Ms. Wright:

As President of XYZ Company, I hereby fully support the project's objectives and proposed training outcomes as stated in your January 24 Summary Memorandum. Along with this commitment is the agreed-upon availability of resources as requested.

With all best wishes for success, I remain,

Sincerely,

Philip Phillips
President

☑ DETERMINE SKILLS, KNOWLEDGE AND ATTITUDES

In some circumstances, the problem that management identified may not be a training problem. So as not to waste training time, money and other resources, you need to determine people's skills, knowledge and attitudes (SKAs) to determine if they relate to a training problem.

As you conduct your needs analysis, investigating SKAs is critical. Explore the following factors that cause performance problems:

✓ Lack of Skills and Knowledge to Do the Job

Can employees do the tasks needed to meet the performance goals? If the answer is yes, there is no training problem and some other intervention should be considered.

✓ Lack of Specific Standards or Job Expectations

Do employees know and understand their performance expectations?

✓ Lack of Feedback

Do employees receive feedback about their performance?

✓ Lack of Necessary Resources to Perform

Do employees have everything they need to perform?

✓ Lack of Appropriate Consequences for Performance

Do employees receive appropriate incentives to perform adequately?

☑ DEFINE CONTENT AREAS

One of your major responsibilities is to compile a list of needs and ideas for training activities. Several methods are available for developing this list. For starters, you can conduct a formal needs analysis, respond to a request from a specific unit or assist with training on some newly installed equipment.

Continually add data and information to the files begun in Step 1: Surveillance. By keeping this master file system up to date with related data whenever a training or performance issue arises, you will have background information and a clearer idea of how issues have evolved.

☑ COLLECT AND ORGANIZE DATA

When a performance problem exists or an organizational need surfaces, the first thought that pops into people's heads is to "train the problem away." However, methods other than training should also be considered. Before thinking about a training program, you must determine if training is the appropriate intervention.

There are other good reasons to conduct a needs analysis before actually developing a training program. When you design training activities, it is extremely helpful to obtain case material directly from the workplace or participants' personal situations. Armed with this information, you can base your designs on real issues that participants face rather than on simulated material.

As you think about the kind of information that would be useful, consider first asking the potential participants to identify their needs. Going directly to the participants for the information gives them a role in designing and developing their own program. Moreover, involving them at this stage is usually appreciated and well received and increases the program's likelihood of success.

Collecting information in this way prior to training allows for developing a possible relationship with the participants and their supervisors and managers. If you cannot collect information directly from each person in your target audience, consider the following two options:

▶ Send a questionnaire to participants before meeting them—this provides an opportunity to tell them about yourself and your plans for the upcoming program and to learn about them.

▶ Phone or visit some or all of the participants for an interview—this provides the opportunity for face-to-face interaction and minimizes feeling awkward should you later meet in the classroom.

The sample Audience Analysis Profile on page 45 will help you formulate your questions and record employees' answers. Their responses will help you complete the Problem Analysis Profile (see sample on page 57).

Sample Audience Analysis Profile

Name: _____

Date: _____

Issue: _____

Area	Questions	Answers
Education	Range of school experience	*High school diploma*
	Native language	*English*
	Average reading level	*12th grade*
Work Experience	Existing skills or knowledge related to proposed training	*Newly hired, no previous training*
	Variation of work experience levels	*Basic skills*
Training	Motivation	*Eager, wants training*
	Recent training experience	*Basic departmental orientation*
	Effect on current job	*Needs training to progress*
	Degree of accountability	*Must attend or not attend*
Implementation	Number of people to be trained	*Three*
	Location of people to be trained	*Conference room B*

CASE STUDY: Step ② Investigation

Lorraine's investigation verifies that several needs exist:

- Organizational Need—Establish a common understanding among management and staff about how the adult and children's programs meet the Club's unique market niche.

- Performance Need—Review the performance rehearsals schedule to develop a more efficient and effective one.

- Problem Need—Review the sports activities to determine equipment, personnel and instruction requirements.

Lorraine uses the organizational, performance and problem profile sheets to document her findings. Next, she reviews her findings with the Training Committee. After receiving their input, Lorraine prepares for her meeting with management at which she will review the preliminary data and the proposed training objectives and outcomes.

After receiving management support to continue the project, Lorraine again meets with the Training Committee. Together, the group completes the Data Summary Sheet Organizer, which documents the source of the problem, the evidence needed, the skill sets involved, the priority and whether the problem is a training or an educational issue.

The group must also decide which data collection methodology to use. It selects a two-tiered data collection approach including an all-staff survey, a guest questionnaire and one-on-one interviews. Collecting these data provides Lorraine with the information she needs to make an informed decision about training intervention.

Next, the Training Committee develops an open-ended survey consisting of two general questions to determine if the interviewed guest's stay was enjoyable and if there were areas that needed improvement. Front desk staff distribute the simple, one-page questionnaire to guests to complete during their stay. To guarantee a high return, management agrees to provide a tee-shirt to every guest who responds.

To collect data, management and staff customize the Interview Guide. Staff interviews are to be conducted the following week.

III

Analysis

WHAT IS ANALYSIS?

The analysis step is the assessment process that provides a clear picture of the problem, the evidence and the data sources. Three types of analysis—goal, organization, job—help determine the type of problem. Using the tools for recording and presenting the findings of the analyses makes it easy for all involved to visualize the problem or performance gap.

Upon completing the analysis step, you can readily determine the best solution—using in-house personnel, hiring consultants or purchasing a complete package.

☑ DECIDE WHETHER TRAINING IS APPROPRIATE

Until now, your primary focus has been on identifying the need, its possible causes and alternative solutions. Now the question becomes how to solve the identified problem. To determine whether training or another solution can solve the problem, you must accurately assess its root cause. This is the most critical stage of the needs analysis process.

If the issue is caused by a lack of information, knowledge or skill, training can redress the problem. If the problem is a result of poor communication, lack of feedback, inadequate supervision, inappropriate or inadequate rewards, or inferior procedures, training is not the answer. You must investigate further to ensure that other issues are not responsible, in whole or in part, for the problem.

If training is a viable solution to the problem, the analysis should include the critical knowledge, skills and attitudes required for optimal performance and an appropriate training and development strategy.

Thus **Step 3: Analysis** has three purposes:

> **1.** Confirm the need for a training program.
>
> **2.** Select the methodology for developing the training program.
>
> **3.** Establish what participants need to learn.

In order to get the most from your analysis, you need to know something about the training process so you can evaluate your data accurately. This is especially important when the person doing the needs analysis is not a professional trainer (e.g., the person is a manager or supervisor).

TYPES OF TRAINING NEEDS

Organizing the Data

There are two types of training needs—macro and micro. A micro training need is one that exists for just one person or for a very small population. A macro training need is one that exists for a large group of employees, frequently for the entire population with the same job classifications. Consider both macro and micro needs when planning training activities.

Three Sources of Training Needs

The three primary sources of training needs are people, the job and the organization. A source internal to the organization means that someone or something within your organization brings the issue to your attention. A source external to the organization means that a person, place or thing outside your organization reveals the issue.

Often the first sign that training might be needed surfaces as a specific problem within one of the three primary sources. Once you are aware of the issue, you must decide whether it is:

- Performance related

- Short- or long-term

- New or recurring

- Affecting a few or many employees

- Urgent, important or unimportant

Use the Data Summary Sheet: How to Determine if Training is Appropriate on page 53 to guide your decision about the appropriateness of training to resolve the issue.

Now that you've determined that training is appropriate, it's time to analyze the data you collected in Step 2: Investigation. This analysis will help you develop the most effective training program possible.

TYPES OF TRAINING NEEDS (continued)

Sources of Training Needs		
Source	Internal to Organization	External to Organization
People	Potential trainers Supervisors Upper-level managers	Trainers in other organizations Consultants
Job	Personnel changes (new hires, promotions) Job task changes Changes in performance standards Equipment changes Analyses of efficiency indexes (e.g., waste, down time, repairs, quality control)	Professional associations Consultants Government regulations
Organization	Changes in the organization's mission Mergers and acquisitions Change in organization structure New products and services Analysis of organizational climate (e.g., grievances, absenteeism, turnover, accidents)	Government regulations and legislative mandates Outside consultants Pressure from competition Environmental pressures (e.g., political, economic, demographic, technical)

Based on the work of Laird (1985) and Nadler (1982).

DATA SUMMARY SHEET
How to Determine if Training is Appropriate

1. Outline the problem or need in the organization for which you believe training might be appropriate. Be as specific as possible.

2. Is this a macro or micro problem or need? What action are you suggesting?

3. Determine whether the need or problem you have identified is performance-related and why or why not. If the need or problem is performance-related, go to number 4. If the need or problem is not performance-related, go to number 5.

4. Classify the need or problem you have identified as something the employees (check one):

   ❏ Do not know (lack of knowledge)

   ❏ Cannot do (lack of skill)

   ❏ Can do, but aren't motivated to do

   If it is a lack of skill or knowledge, then a training activity is an appropriate intervention. If you have classified it as a lack of motivation, go to number 5.

5. Identify possible alternative solutions (other than training) to the problem or need you have identified. List these alternatives.

☑ THREE TYPES OF ANALYSIS

> ✓ Goal
>
> ✓ Organizational
>
> ✓ Job

Which method you choose depends upon the category of problem your training program must address.

GOAL ANALYSIS

Use goal analysis when developing a training program whose objective is to correct a performance problem or when training is not oriented toward a specific job or position (e.g., professional development programs). Goal analysis is also important when training programs are charged with developing people to serve in new positions, when they attempt to instill or alter a corporate culture, or when they need to change attitudes or beliefs.

Goal analysis requires that you identify key organizational objectives and their behavioral indicators. Behavioral indicators are the abstract qualities (such as feelings) that help a person perform well or badly in a particular position. They provide a baseline against which to measure improvement. Goal analysis ends when you have a complete list of behavioral indicators for each goal.

Sample Goal Analysis

Goal: A project manager should be a self-starter.

Behavioral indicators:

- Completes assignments on time without reminders.
- Initiates requests for new assignments on completing assignments.
- Takes responsibility for getting the work done.
- Requests duties with responsibility.

ORGANIZATIONAL ANALYSIS

Organizational analysis means gathering information to solve a problem involving the makeup of a company. By answering the following questions you ensure that the training supports the required performance standards:

Q. What are the organization's business goals?

Q. What are the organization's key products?

Q. How is the organization structured?

Q. What are the roles and responsibilities of staff within the organization?

Q. What resources are available?

Q. What perceived needs or problems do organization members express?

Q. What is the typical way that people are trained in the organization?

While these questionnaires can be valuable tools in building an effective training program, they do have their drawbacks. Don't forget to consider *all* of the information you have gathered. The Data Summary Sheet Organizer on page 59 will help you pull it all together before you proceed to Step 3: Analysis.

Sample Problem Analysis Profile

Name: _____

Date: _____

Issue: _____

Performance Area _____

_____

Performance Goal _____

_____

Current Performance _____

_____

Gap Between Goal
and Performance _____

_____

Causes	Findings
Do employees have the skills and knowledge to meet performance goals?	*No*
Do employees know performance standards or expectations?	*Varies among individuals*
Do employees receive feedback about their performance?	*Yes, generally only negative responses when things go wrong*
Do employees have the necessary resources to perform?	*Yes, but they need training in how to use them effectively*
Do employees receive appropriate incentives to perform?	*No*

ORGANIZATIONAL ANALYSIS (continued)

Advantages and Disadvantages of Questionnaires		
Types of Questionnaire	**Advantages**	**Disadvantages**
• Survey or poll of a random or specific sample of respondents, or of an entire "population."	• Reach a large number of people in a short time.	• Little provision for free expression of unanticipated responses.
• Contains a variety of question formats —open-ended, projective, forced-choice, priority-ranking.	• Relatively inexpensive to produce.	• Require substantial time (and technical skills, especially in survey model) for developing effective questions and analyzing responses.
• May use rating scales, either predesigned or self-generated by respondent(s).	• Anonymous questionnaires and surveys provide opportunity for expressing self without fear of embarrassment or recrimination.	• Are of limited utility in getting at causes of problems or possible solutions.
• May be self-administered (by mail) under controlled or uncontrolled conditions, or may require the presence of an interpreter or assistant.	• Yield data that can be easily summarized and reported.	• Suffer low return rates (mailed), grudging responses, or unintended and/ or inappropriate respondents.

This chart is based on the work of Mel Silberman, *Active Training,* Addison-Wesley, 1996.

Data Summary Sheet Organizer				
Source	**Evidence of Need**	**Skills Set(s)**	**Previous Education or Training**	**Priority**
Organization				
People				
Job				

ORGANIZATIONAL ANALYSIS (continued)

Q. What general problems exist within the organization that may affect the training program?

Sample Organizational Analysis
Issue: Job roles are not clearly defined within a given department.

Ways to clarify roles:

- Organization chart

- Roles/responsibility matrix

- Description of problems and training needs by position

JOB ANALYSIS

Job analysis involves recording information about a particular job and breaking it down into tasks to pinpoint where the training or performance need exists. Start by reviewing job literature, observing job performance and questioning people on the job. The Job Analysis Questionnaire on page 62 can substitute for face-to-face interviewing or serve as a guide when conducting the interviews.

After you have surveyed a representative sample of your training audience, summarize their responses on the Job Analysis Profile. This gives you a general overview of what's happening—or not—among groups of people with the same job title.

After breaking down the functional responsibilities into tasks, validate the job analysis with an advisory group (subject matter experts, management representatives, client contacts) to guarantee that the job analysis matches the job. Then ask the advisory group to help select the key functions and tasks that will be the focus of your training course. Selecting key tasks is often necessary because there is not enough time to prepare training for everything that was uncovered in a job analysis.

Now you will be able to analyze those tasks identified as the focus of your training.

Remember, even with careful observation during a job analysis, relevant abstract qualities may not surface. Nevertheless, their effects are noticeable in how well people do the job, so you should take them into account when designing a training program.

Job Analysis Questionnaire

Task	Frequency	How Did You Learn to Do It?	Rate Its Importance Compared to Your Overall Responsibilities			What's the Best Way to Learn this Task?
_____	Daily Weekly Monthly Other	On Job School Training Other	High	Average	Low	On Job School Training Other
_____	Daily Weekly Monthly Other	On Job School Training Other	High	Average	Low	On Job School Training Other
_____	Daily Weekly Monthly Other	On Job School Training Other	High	Average	Low	On Job School Training Other
_____	Daily Weekly Monthly Other	On Job School Training Other	High	Average	Low	On Job School Training Other
_____	Daily Weekly Monthly Other	On Job School Training Other	High	Average	Low	On Job School Training Other
_____	Daily Weekly Monthly Other	On Job School Training Other	High	Average	Low	On Job School Training Other
_____	Daily Weekly Monthly Other	On Job School Training Other	High	Average	Low	On Job School Training Other
_____	Daily Weekly Monthly Other	On Job School Training Other	High	Average	Low	On Job School Training Other
_____	Daily Weekly Monthly Other	On Job School Training Other	High	Average	Low	On Job School Training Other
_____	Daily Weekly Monthly Other	On Job School Training Other	High	Average	Low	On Job School Training Other
_____	Daily Weekly Monthly Other	On Job School Training Other	High	Average	Low	On Job School Training Other
_____	Daily Weekly Monthly Other	On Job School Training Other	High	Average	Low	On Job School Training Other

Adapted from Geri McArdle TSA.

Job Analysis Profile Sheet

Job Title of Training Audience _____

Functional Responsibilities	Tasks Involved in Each
(A collection of related tasks that focus on one area of an individual's job, such as managing the benefits program)	(Individual performance elements that produce and identify product, such as updating the HR database)

☑ PRESENT FINDINGS

Three good ways to present your findings are check sheets, line graphs and Pareto charts.

Examples of each follow.

Check Sheets

Check sheets, which are easy to design and use, use hash marks to show the frequency of a number of events. Beginning with a check sheet allows you to decide what events to record, determine the time period for the observation (e.g., hours, days, months) and develop the format. Information from check sheets is easily transferable to a frequency graph.

Sample Check Sheet					
	September				
Delay	**3**	**4**	**5**	**6**	**Total**
Missing information	II	I	III	II	8
Policy changes/questions	THL	THL II	IIII	THL III	24
Input errors	THL IIII	THL THL III	THL II	THL IIII	38
Alerts/routing		I	II	I	4
Individual work habits	II	III	II	III	10
Total	**18**	**25**	**18**	**23**	**84**

From Society for Human Resource Management, Alexandria, VA.

Line Graphs

A line graph displays trends in a particular activity over a specific time period. Use the line graph to track a specific activity over a period of time to identify changes as soon as they occur. By noting the change immediately, you can recommend taking prompt action.

Pareto Charts

A Pareto chart is a bar graph. The bar graph displays the relative importance of different events or needs. The most frequent events or greatest needs (the higher numbers) appear to the left of the chart. The Pareto chart is similar to the check sheet in its ability to identify root causes of problems.

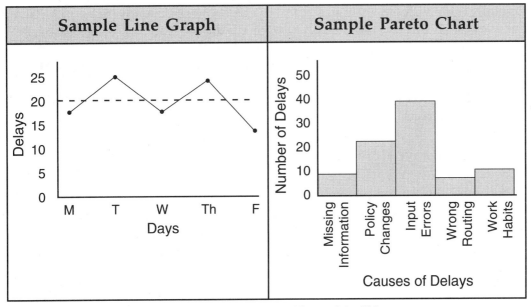

Sample Line Graph	Sample Pareto Chart

From Society for Human Resource Management, Alexandria, VA

☑ CHOOSE TRAINERS

Once the organization has developed a clear picture of the training priorities, the next step is to decide the best way to meet the needs. The organization can design, develop and deliver the training program in-house; it can contract with an outside consultant to design and develop the coursework for in-house delivery; it can contract with an outside training facility to handle all aspects of the training; or it can purchase a commercially marketed training program and train in-house staff to teach the program.

Organizations without in-house training departments usually have to look outside for all but the most basic type of on-the-job training programs. For organizations that do have internal training staff, the decision is more complex. Answers to the following questions can help narrow the choice:

Q. How often and to how many employees will the training program be offered?

Q. Do we have a content expert with credible delivery skills?

Q. Will the training program address a one-time need targeted to only a few employees or will the program take place a few times a year?

Q. Will training involve generic skills or a specific technical need?

Q. Will the trainees be lower-level staff or upper-level managers?

Q. Will the content of the program involve proprietary or competitive information?

In thinking about the questions, you might consider cost effectiveness. If training will be infrequent, using an outside consultant may be more cost effective. Alternatively, ongoing training needed by many employees may be more cost effective if developed and delivered in-house. When training involves technology, equipment or skills unique to the organization and its jobs, in-house design and delivery may be the only option. For top management, a consultant's polished presentation and broad range of experience with other companies may enhance the program's credibility. For lower-level positions, trainees may view a program as more relevant and credible if it is developed and delivered by someone familiar with day-to-day problems. If the content of the training program is proprietary, again, developing and delivering the program in-house is probably preferred.

Using In-House Personnel

For many types of training, qualified course instructors can be found within the organization. Each executive, for instance, has expertise in a certain area, and most can make time to conduct at least one or two training sessions. Other potential instructors include supervisors and managers; human resource personnel, especially those with career counseling and similar experience; and professional employees, particularly ones who have had previous teaching experience.

Hiring Outside Trainers

Part- and full-time faculty at area colleges and universities are ideal candidates to recruit as trainers. Depending on the nature of the course, other outside professionals to consider as instructors or guest speakers include consultants, lawyers, psychologists, systems analysts or efficiency experts. Professional and trade associations, as well as local chambers of commerce, may have the names of experts willing to make presentations.

☑ CLARIFY TRAINING OBJECTIVES

Training program objectives should be clearly stated to ensure they include those critical activities or performance issues that will be accepted as evidence that the participants learned something.

There are two types of objectives:

► Terminal

Statements that describe what a training program participant will be able to do at the end of the training program, under what conditions and at what level of competence. Terminal objectives are the cornerstone of a training program because training program developers, instructors, participants, clients and evaluators all use them.

► Enabling

Fluid parts that flow from the major task statements (e.g., output, nature of the organization). These type of objectives represent the basic skills, knowledge and attitudes that must be learned before meeting the instructional objective.

☑ DESIGN TRAINING AND COURSE MODULE

The instructional specifications, guidelines for content, timing of presentation of ideas and reasons content are included, serving as a blueprint for program development. The completed program can then be compared to the blueprint when the training course is evaluated.

Specifying instructional content is a joint effort by training and subject matter experts. In this part of the analysis, the trainers and experts will define the critical content of each course module. They will also decide which strategies to use when introducing the content, determining appropriate learning techniques, providing opportunities for practice and incorporating the appropriate media forms.

The last stage of Step 3: Analysis is to develop a sample training module to include in the Training Design Report, which you will complete in Step 4: Report. The example 30-minute training module that follows is designed to teach someone how to record a message on an answering machine. (Rosemary Bhrem, Learning Partners, Tampa, Florida, developed the example.)

Sample Module Design		
Module Name: Recording Answering Machine Greetings		
Objective	**Content**	**Instructor/Learner Activities**
Given an answering machine with recording tape and a procedures manual, the learner will record a greeting into the machine so that when a call is received the recording plays in the allotted time.	► Parts of an answering machine ► Length of message ► Components of a message ► Steps to record a message	► Overhead visual of answering machine and its parts ► Instructor presents examples of recorded greetings ► Learners write their greetings ► Learners time their greetings ► Learners adjust greetings to fit allotted time ► Instructor demonstrates how to record greeting ► Learners record greetings

Module Design Profile Sheet		
Module Name:		
Objective	Content	Instructor/Learner Activities

(Create as many as needed to complete your Module Design.)

CASE STUDY: Step ③ Analysis

Until now, Lorraine and the Training Committee have concentrated their efforts on identifying the needs and possible causes and on generating alternative preliminary solutions. Now the group is ready to determine how the identified organizational performance and problem needs can be solved. To do this, the group must accurately assess the root causes for each need.

Lorraine knows that if a lack of information, knowledge or skill causes a problem, then training can redress it. She also knows that if the problem results from poor communication or lack of results, training is not necessarily the appropriate intervention.

Lorraine has sorted and categorized the topics or themes from the information she gathered from the guest surveys and management and staff interviews. Results indicate that problems do exist: on the organizational level—lack of sports equipment; on the performance level—lack of adequate training and certification in water sports; and on the problem level—lack of knowledge concerning the goal and objectives of the Club's children's program.

Lorraine uses several tools to present the findings: a check sheet to indicate how many times in one week guests engaged in particular sports activities; a line graph to display the same data; and a Pareto chart to show the relative importance of different sports events and the need for certification and equipment.

Lorraine decides she will propose two training interventions: a training program and certification process for all water sports staff and an orientation program management would present to all staff explaining the evolution of the children's program, the Club's market niche, and the roles and responsibilities required to support the adult and children's programs. Lorraine delegates to the Vice President for Club Operations and Activities the performance rehearsal schedule issue, which is an operational, not a training, issue.

IV

Report

REPORTING YOUR FINDINGS

Two types of reports communicate the results of the needs analysis process—a Training Design Report and a Final Report.

The Training Design Report summarizes the investigation and analysis findings, presents recommendations and suggests material the training manager should use for each stage of the project.

The Final Report identifies performance gaps and what needs to be changed, how changes will be made and how the changes fit into the organization's goals. Consider the Final Report as a sales presentation to management that states the needs and provides the business justification for using training intervention to address the needs.

Communicating the results from both report phases verbally and orally usually improves chances for success.

TRAINING DESIGN REPORT

Written in simple, clear language and assuming a wide audience, many of whom may not be familiar with the topic, the Training Design Report describes the results of the investigation and analysis, communicates progress to key management and provides the training manager with material for supervising each stage of the project. Use the sample on page 77 as a guide.

The following eight components comprise the training design report:

► ## *Purpose of Proposed Course*

Describes the training problem, the training format and the history of the problem within the organization. This section should be one paragraph.

► ## *Summary of Analysis*

Summarizes the need; clearly defines the performance gaps that the proposed training will address; describes the audience; and describes the job, the tasks that make up that job and the key performance elements needed to fulfill the job requirements. This extensive description is necessary because the performance gap is probably located in a task, in a performance element of the task, or in a lack or misunderstanding of the knowledge the participants need to perform the task.

► ## *Scope of the Course*

Establishes the format for the course. Presents an overview of the materials the trainer will use, the content he or she will cover and the instructional strategies he or she will employ to deliver the course.

► ## *Learning Objectives*

Presents the learning objective statements that will guide the course and the learning.

► ## *Test Item Strategy*

Describes how the participants will demonstrate mastery of the topic. Explains how you will conduct the testing and why and what happens after the testing. For example, if the participants fail a test item, you should decide whether the test item should be rewritten or whether the training materials are problematic.

► *Course and Module Design*

Establishes a blueprint for your training program and includes: course and module title; learning objectives; course content and instructor/learner activities that are designed to bring about mastery of the learning objectives.

► *Delivery Strategy*

Describes the instructional methods; the length of the course; and the training format, timing and location.

► *Evaluation or Measurement Tools*

Explains your evaluation mechanism and how you are going to measure the participants' reactions to the training, their learning (the results of the test items) and their behavior (how the concepts mastered will be translated back to the job).

Sample Training Design Report
Purpose of proposed course
Summary of analysis
Scope of the course
Learning objectives
Test item strategy
Course and module design
Delivery strategy
Evaluation or measurement tools

FINAL REPORT

Again, using clear, concise language, the final report presents the results of all phases of the needs analysis and discusses how your findings relate to the organization's overall strategy and goals. The report will identify performance gaps between the position in question and the function of the position as defined. It paints the complete picture of what needs to be changed, how changes will be made and how the organization and individuals will be affected by the changes. Think of this report as the final sales presentation to all levels of the organization.

The following nine components comprise the final report:

► *Executive Summary*

This first section is among the most crucial. The executive summary should be short. One page is ideal, and certainly not more than two pages. It answers the question: "If readers are too busy to look at the entire report, what's the least amount of information they need to make an informed decision?"

► *Objectives of the Needs Analysis*

Explains in detail the objectives of the needs analysis. What information did you hope to learn?

► *Brief Summary of Findings*

Discusses optimal performance (what the organization hopes to achieve), actual performance (the organization's current level of performance), and how to bridge the gap between the two.

► *Proposed Change or Training Project*

Explains clearly the commitment involved. How much will the program cost? How long will it take to complete? How long before we see results? Who will be involved? How will the program be implemented? What resources are needed for the program to succeed?

► *Data Collection Methods*

Explains why you collected the data you did and the process you used to analyze data and information.

► *Expanded Discussion of Findings*

Discusses study results in detail. However, unless you have prepared the presentation for highly analytical thinkers, you may want to present findings in a descriptive form. You can include simple tables and graphs, but also describe the results in words. Save copies of the actual questionnaires for an appendix to the report.

► *Implications and Analysis*

Discusses the implications of your results. Show how the data relate to the organization's objectives.

► *Recommendations for Future Action*

Presents specific recommendations for future action. Recommendations should include at least the skills, knowledge and attitudes required for a particular position; a training strategy (what a training program might look like—a module design in graphic form); and other issues you uncovered that management should resolve before proceeding.

► *Appendices of Supporting Data*

Includes relevant supporting data such as sample surveys and other data collection methods, detailed analysis of the results, a cost breakdown and a time line of the proposed change.

FINAL REPORT (continued)

Sample Final Report
Executive summary
Objective of the needs assessment
Brief summary of findings
Proposed change or training project
Data collection methods
Expanded discussion of findings
Implications and analysis
Recommendations for future action
Appendices of supporting data

☑ MAKE ORAL PRESENTATION

When presenting your findings orally, knowing your audience is critical. As much as possible, learn about their values, attitudes and needs. The presentation should focus on answering the question: What's in it for me?

A few tips for 35 mm slides, computer shows or overhead transparencies (all called "frame" in this discussion):

- Limit words per frame.

- Use pleasing and easy-to-see colors (e.g., use blue as foreground or background; don't use yellow, which fades, or red, which is difficult to read).

- Use bulleted lists.

- Use readable graphic images.

- Keep charts and graphs simple.

You, not the frames, are the show. The oral presentation reinforces the material provided in the written reports.

Even if you prepare the "perfect" presentation, that does not mean it will be totally accepted immediately. You may face opposition for any number of reasons. Perhaps the opposing staff member does not see the value in the proposed change. Maybe she or he fears change. Or, maybe she or he recognizes change is necessary but sees a better way than yours.

The best way to overcome an objection is to diffuse it before it is ever raised. Before making your presentation, play Devil's advocate. Review your proposal with a critical eye. Raise any objections you can think of, legitimate or not (however, you may want to steer away from the ridiculous). State each possible objection as if it were a valid criticism of your idea. Then, systematically and logically dismantle each one. This keeps potential dissenters in the role of spectators and allows you to remain in control.

CASE STUDY: Step ④ Report

Once the organization has a clear picture of the training needs, the next step is deciding how best to meet the identified needs. Therefore, Lorraine and the Training Committee are responsible for reporting and recommending the "next step" to management. Establishing management support for training is essential to the success of any training intervention.

Lorraine and the Training Committee decide to develop two presentations. One will be a written report using the Training Design Report format; the other, an oral presentation. Once senior management establishes priorities, Lorraine and the committee decide how to design, develop and deliver the training, using the following questions to narrow their choices:

- How often and to how many employees will the training programs be offered, especially the water sports certification?

- Does the Club have a content expert in water sports who has credible delivery skills and can certify trainees?

- How can an orientation program best be delivered to all Club sites and to all staff members at each site?

- Should proprietary or competitive information be included in the orientation training program?

In thinking about these questions, Lorraine and the Committee realize cost-effectiveness is an important issue, which they will discuss in terms of using in-house personnel or contracting out the training design and delivery, determining which instructional methods to use and developing a training schedule.

Ongoing Issues
in Needs Analysis

EVALUATING THE PROCESS AFTER IMPLEMENTATION

Now you have conducted your needs analysis. You have prepared and distributed surveys, interviewed staff members, compiled and analyzed the data, identified the best change, presented your findings and won over some pretty critical colleagues. So you're finished, right? *Wrong.*

Whatever improvement you have identified, continuing to collect and analyze data is important. You may want to use the same data collection methods you used during the initial stages or develop different methods. Perhaps you will want to use a combination of both.

Set up a Pilot Program

You may even want to set up a pilot program before implementing the change or training strategy throughout the entire organization. If you choose to set up a pilot program, be sure the participants you select are representative of the entire group.

Next, answer the following questions to determine the validity of the change or training model.

Q. Did participants master the necessary information?

Q. What is their perception of the value of the training program?

Q. What are their coworkers' and management's perception of the value of the training?

EVALUATING THE PROCESS AFTER IMPLEMENTATION (continued)

Information that you learn from your pilot group may help you refine the process before presenting it to the organization as a whole. In addition, by continuing to collect data you will be able to:

- Determine whether the training is having the desired results. If not, you may be able to identify the reason and alter the process to achieve the organization's objectives.

- Establish early on if the issue you were asked to address is merely a symptom of a more deeply rooted problem.

- Chart the organization's progress if you are asked at a later date to justify the program.

- Take a proactive stand, not a reactive one, spotting potential problems before they get out of hand.

Ultimately, you will have hard evidence of the program's effectiveness in dealing with the challenge the organization was facing, which, in turn, can make it easier for the organization to become a learning organization.

OVERCOMING OBSTACLES

When conducting a needs analysis of an organization, be prepared to face obstacles: perhaps just a few, perhaps many, perhaps minor, perhaps severe. Your best defense is a good offense—be prepared.

In her 1990 article "Overcoming Obstacles to Needs Assessment," Allison Rossett identifies the root causes of obstacles in the needs analysis process:

> The first root cause is a flawed needs assessment. Perhaps there simply is not enough time nor resources to conduct an adequate needs assessment. The best way to overcome this obstacle is to be certain that you are seeking the correct information. Be sure you address what the organization considers to be optimal performance. Also be sure that you uncover accurate information about the actual level of performance. Ask how the employees and management really feel about the program. Do they see value in changing it?

> Perhaps management believes they understand the issues clearly and that conducting a needs assessment is unnecessary. This leads to the second root cause: lack of organizational support for the needs assessment. To increase the level of support for the program, start documenting what you have learned and how it relates to the organization's bottom line.

> In doing all this, you will be able to answer the ever important question: "What can this program do to help us realize our full potential as individuals and as an organization?"

HOW TO GET TOP MANAGEMENT SUPPORT

As a trainer, you need top-level support to get your job done. Unlike other departments that want top management support yet can function without it, training education and professional development can't, especially in the areas of organization change and developing management staff for the organization.

Top support is not a speech or a memo. Top support is a total organization philosophy. It's declaring that the organization will be a learning organization, and that continuous quality improvements are made through continuous learning.

What is Top Management Support?

Management support is evidenced by consistent words and actions that reflect a strong personal commitment. Managers who support training will constantly refer to the importance of training and a learning organization in speech after speech and meeting after meeting. Managers will continually ask how training and development is working in their visits throughout the organization, will contribute to the training newsletter and courseworks and will probably devote space to training in the annual report.

Management support does not happen overnight. Managers must consistently reward and praise supervisors for developing their staff. The greater the number of supervisors on board and the more resources devoted to professional development, the stronger the belief that management is serious about training.

Indicators that management is serious about training are when you see managers:

- Take an interest in thoughtfully completing, on time, performance appraisals that include individual training plans

- Begin to think about cross-training and identifying and developing back-ups

- Endorse their staff's participation in seminars, university courses, in-house workshops and other development activities and promote staff participation in transfers, task forces, special projects, and on-loan assignments

How Do You Get Support?

William Yeomans, while manager of training and development at the J. C. Penney Company, suggested six ways:

1. *Start thinking of training and development as part of the business.*

Discard the notion that training and development are separate from the organization. Training and development must mesh with and be an integral part of the operation. If you want attention, begin with those programs and activities that help the organization meet its objectives. Obtain a copy of the organization's strategic plan. Review the plan for opportunities that might call for a training or development intervention. Meet with key managers and find out their plans. Determine where the company will need training support and begin with high-priority and high-impact work. Look for new technology, organization changes, new product lines and new organization direction.

2. *Learn the business!*

If you want to "walk the talk" you must know what you are talking about. If you are to talk coherently with managers about what is happening, you had better learn the business, especially the financial end. Many staff people don't bother to do that. For example, do you know what the organization's earnings per share were last year? Do you know the net profit? Do you know the contribution of the major division? Take a course and get to know the financial people so that you can get comfortable with financial objectives, return on investment and sales figures, debt-equity and cash flow. Then, go back to those strategic plans to make sure you understand the "what" and "how" of the new business venture or organizational direction.

HOW TO GET TOP MANAGEMENT SUPPORT
(continued)

3. *Develop programs and activities that line managers want and that satisfy their needs.*

Start with department managers; worry about staff departments later. Use your study of strategic plans and operating reports and your discussion with managers as starting points. In your discussion of need with managers, you can and should give guidance about what training you think is necessary. Be sure whatever you do reflects what the managers really want and need.

4. *Involve top management.*

Ask them which needs are most important. After you've completed your survey at all levels, develop a master plan covering level or general types of training. Your plan should encompass all activities either in place or to be developed. Obtain top management's agreement and get them involved in the training and development process by offering them an opportunity to help train.

5. *Develop practical, how-to programs.*

These types of programs give people tools they can use on the job immediately. Move away from any academic image you may have. Stay clear of theory and fads. Only after job training is in place can you move to "hot" topics.

6. *Get a handle on return on investment (ROI).*

ROI is an important part of doing business. Becoming involved in ROI includes identifying existing programs or activities that have a direct measurable effect on performance. Design evaluations of those training programs and carry them out. Use before and after results to compare groups and measure the effect of training and savings. Use long periods of time to compare results (e.g., six months). Once you have accumulated some meaningful statistics, publish the results. This illustrates that your programs have a positive effect and that you are concerned with ROI.

These six steps are not easy to implement. They take time and a well-developed plan to establish and monitor. However, taking the steps is certainly possible, and the rewards are there for the asking. Organizational alignment and productive people in the right jobs are only a few of the outcomes.

CONTINUOUS NEEDS ANALYSIS

An effective training department must continually plan, design, deliver and assess its training intervention. The following steps provide a useful strategy.

STEP ①: Assess Ongoing Training

What training do employees need? What new skills will the organization need in the future? Conduct an annual needs survey. Rank the identified needs and concentrate on those first by developing a six-month or year-long training agenda.

Some typical categories of training topics:

► Health and safety topics

► Sales and customer service training

► Clerical, technical, and specialized, interpersonal, or managerial skills

► Professional advancement programs such as career and personal development

► Succession planning

STEP ②: Designing Training Programs

Determine the following for each training program you develop:

► Course objectives

► Test items

► Instructional methods

► Material content

CONTINUOUS NEEDS ANALYSIS (continued)

► Course and module design

► Training program length

► Method for identifying participants

► Trainer and program manager

► Budget

► Training announcement

► Registration and confirmation process

STEP ③: Design Training Course, Sample Module and Course Module

Before beginning the training program, sell the program to employees and management. Meet with selected instructors to ensure the training goal is consistent with your design and instructional methodology. Check the materials, logistics and evaluation mechanism.

STEP ④: Create the Training Report

Before beginning to design a training intervention, you must describe clearly your training concept and secure management's approval.

STEP ⑤: Return to Step 1

WHAT TO DO WHEN THERE IS NO TIME TO CONDUCT A NEEDS ANALYSIS

Following are some suggestions for obtaining information quickly:

- Phone a contact person who is familiar with the participants. Use the audience analysis and the problem analysis profile sheet.

- Introduce yourself and ask participants some key questions via telephone. Again, use the profile sheets in Step 2: Investigation. Trust the responses to be representative and treat them as if they were a sample of the large group. Or, ask a contact person to schedule a phone interview for you.

- Ensure that you receive relevant materials (e.g., surveys, meeting notes, records).

- Obtain opinions and impressions from other trainers who have worked with the training group.

- Talk to participants who arrive early and obtain whatever information you can.

- Design some activities at the beginning of the program to enable you to assess the group.

If you conducted some front-end assessment and designed your program based on your assessment results, you should be able to make final adjustments before the training meeting begins.

REFERENCES

Cummings, Thomas G. and Christopher Worley. *Organization Development and Change.* St. Paul, Minnesota: West Publishing Company, 1996.

Laird, Dugan. *Approaches to Training and Development.* Reading, MA: Addison-Wesley, 1985.

Nadler, Leonard. *Designing Training Programs: The Critical Events Model.* Reading, MA: Addison-Wesley, 1982.

Rossett, Allison. "Overcoming Obstacles to Needs Assessment." *Training: The Magazine of Human Resource Development* (1990) 27(3): 36.

Rossett, Allison. *Training Needs Assessment.* Englewood Cliffs, NJ: Educational Testing Publications, 1987.

Senge, Peter. *The Fifth Discipline.* New York: Doubleday Currency, 1990.

Silberman, Mel. *Active Training.* New York: Lexington Books, 1990.

Yeomans, William. "How to Get Top Management Support." *Training and Development Journal.* Alexandria, Virginia: American Society for Training and Development, 1982.

RESOURCE LIST

Associations

American Management Association
1601 Broadway
New York, New York 10020   212.586.8100

Services: dedicated to the needs of trainers and development organizational managers. Membership privileges: use of library, management information service including a wide data base of articles, books, pamphlets; special publication privileges; discounts on various programs and courses.

American Society for Training and Development
1630 Duke Street
Box 1443
Alexandria, Virginia 22313   800.628.2783

Services: dedicated to the needs of trainers, human resource development professionals. National membership privileges: discounts on publications, conference centers; membership directory, various subscriptions, buyer's guide; library access. Local chapters in major metropolitan areas in the U.S.

International Society for Performance Improvement
1300 L Street NW
Washington, DC 20005   202.408.7969

Services: dedicated to the needs of instructional designers and developers. National membership privileges, publications, discounts on conferences. Local chapters in major metropolitan areas in the U.S.

Business Bookstores

American Management Association
1601 Broadway
New York, New York 10019   212.903.8286

American Society for Training and Development
1630 Duke Street
Alexandria, Virginia 22313   703.683.8100

RESOURCE LIST (continued)

Media Companies

Barr Films
12801 Schatarum Avenue
P.O. Box 7878
Irwindale, California 91706   1.800.234.7878

CRM Films
2233 Faraday Avenue
Carlsbad, California 92008   1.800.421.0833

Publications

The HRD Quarterly
Organization Design and Development
2002 Renaissance Boulevard
Suite 1000
King of Prussia, Pennsylvania 19406   215.279.2002

Management Review (AMA)
1601 Broadway
New York, New York 10019   212.903.8165

Training and Development Literature Index
American Society for Training and Development
1630 Duke Street
Box 1443
Alexandria, Virginia 22313   703.683.8129

Training Magazine
Organization Design and Development
Lakewood Publications 50 S. Ninth Street
Minneapolis, Minnesota 55402   612.333.0471

Trainer's Workshop
American Management Association
1601 Broadway
New York, New York 10019   212.903.8165

NOTES

NOTES

NOTES

NOTES

NOTES

NOTES

NOTES

Now Available From

Books•Videos•CD-ROMs•Computer-Based Training Products

Subject Areas Include:

Management
Human Resources
Communication Skills
Personal Development
Marketing/Sales
Organizational Development
Customer Service/Quality
Computer Skills
Small Business and Entrepreneurship
Adult Literacy and Learning
Life Planning and Retirement

CRISP WORLDWIDE DISTRIBUTION

English language books are distributed worldwide. Major international distributors include:

ASIA/PACIFIC

Australia/New Zealand: In Learning, PO Box 1051, Springwood QLD, Brisbane,
Australia 4127   Tel: 61-7-3-841-2286, Facsimile: 61-7-3-841-2618
ATTN: Messrs. Gordon

Philippines: National Book Store Inc., Quad Alpha Centrum Bldg, 125 Pioneer Street,
Mandaluyong, Metro Manila, Philippines   Tel: 632-631-8051, Facsimile: 632-631-5016

Singapore, Malaysia, Brunei, Indonesia: Times Book Shops. Direct sales HQ:
STP Distributors, Pasir Panjang Distrientre, Block 1 #03-01A, Pasir Panjang Rd,
Singapore 118480   Tel: 65-2767626, Facsimile: 65-2767119

Japan: Phoenix Associates Co., Ltd., Mizuho Bldng, 3-F, 2-12-2, Kami Osaki,
Shinagawa-Ku, Tokyo 141   Tel: 81-33-443-7231, Facsimile: 81-33-443-7640
ATTN: Mr. Peter Owans

CANADA

Crisp Learning Canada, 60 Briarwood Avenue, Mississauga, ON L5G 3N6 Canada
Tel: (905) 274-5678, Facsimile: (905) 278-2801
ATTN: Mr. Steve Connolly/Mr. Jerry McNabb

Trade Book Stores: Raincoast Books, 8680 Cambie Street,
Vancouver, BC V6P 6M9 Canada
Tel: (604) 323-7100, Facsimile: (604) 323-2600   ATTN: Order Desk

EUROPEAN UNION

England: Flex Training, Ltd., 9-15 Hitchin Street,
Baldock, Hertfordshire, SG7 6A, England
Tel: 44-1-46-289-6000, Facsimile: 44-1-46-289-2417   ATTN: Mr. David Willetts

INDIA

Multi-Media HRD, Pvt., Ltd., National House,
Tulloch Road, Appolo Bunder, Bombay, India 400-039
Tel: 91-22-204-2281, Facsimile: 91-22-283-6478   ATTN: Messrs. Aggarwal

SOUTH AMERICA

Mexico: Grupo Editorial Iberoamerica, Nebraska 199, Col. Napoles, 03810 Mexico, D.F.
Tel: 525-523-0994, Facsimile: 525-543-1173   ATTN: Señor Nicholas Grepe

SOUTH AFRICA

Alternative Books, PO Box 1345, Ferndale 2160, South Africa
Tel: 27-11-792-7730, Facsimile: 27-11-792-7787   ATTN: Mr. Vernon de Haas